from SEA TO SHINING SEA

OHIO

By Dennis Brindell Fradin

CONSULTANTS

George W. Knepper, Ph.D., Distinguished Professor of History, Emeritus,
The University of Akron

Robert L. Hillerich, Ph.D., Professor Emeritus, Bowling Green State University;
Consultant, Pinellas County Schools, Florida

CHILDRENS PRESS®
CHICAGO

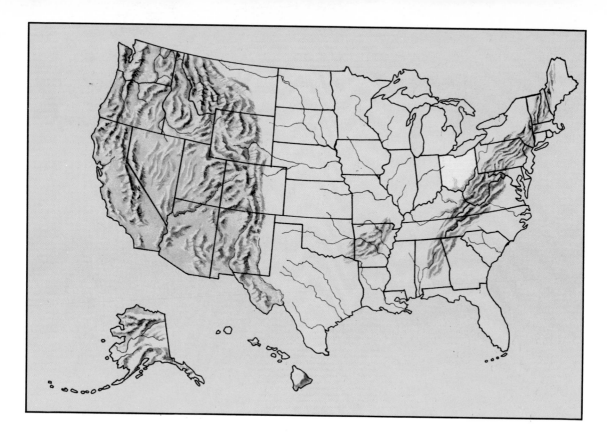

Ohio is one of the twelve states in the region called the Midwest. The other Midwest states are Illinois, Michigan, Wisconsin, Indiana, Iowa, Minnesota, Missouri, Nebraska, North Dakota, South Dakota, and Kansas.

For my editor and friend, Fran Dyra

Front cover picture: a skyline view of Columbus from Bicentennial Park; page 1: the Muskingum River near Dresden; back cover: an Amish farm near Bunker Hill

Project Editor: Joan Downing
Design Director: Karen Kohn
Research Assistant: Judith Bloom Fradin
Typesetting: Graphic Connections, Inc.
Engraving: Liberty Photoengraving

FOURTH PRINTING, 1994.

Library of Congress Cataloging-in-Publication Data

Fradin, Dennis B.
  Ohio / by Dennis Brindell Fradin.
   p.   cm. — (From sea to shining sea)
  Includes index.
  Summary: Introduces the history, geography, industries, notable sights, and famous people of the Buckeye State.
  ISBN 0-516-03835-4
  1. Ohio—Juvenile literature. [1. Ohio.] I. Title.
II. Series: Fradin, Dennis B. From sea to shining sea.
F491.3.F697   1993   92-39796
977.1—dc20   CIP
                                              AC

Table of Contents

Fifth graders, Southdale

"Something Great"

Ohio is a small midwestern state. It is shaped like a waving flag. The name *Ohio* is an Indian word meaning "something great." Ohio was known for its buckeye trees in pioneer times. Ohio is now nicknamed the "Buckeye State." The people of Ohio are called Ohioans. Sometimes they are called Buckeyes.

Ohio lives up to the meaning of its Indian name. The state is a leader in manufacturing, farming, and mining. Many Ohioans have achieved greatness. Seven presidents were born in Ohio. That's why Ohio is called the "Mother of Presidents." Ohio is also called the "Mother of Inventors." The airplane and the electric light were invented by Ohioans.

The Buckeye State is special in other ways. What state has an Indian mound shaped like a giant snake? What state had the first black mayor of a major city? Where do the Reds and Indians play baseball? Where do the Browns and Bengals play football? Where was the first person to walk on the moon born? The answer to these questions is: Ohio!

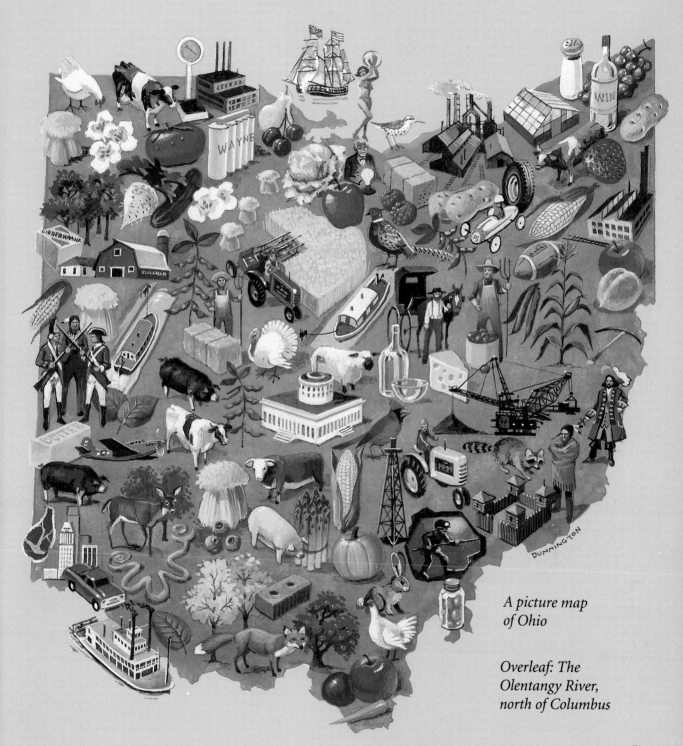

A picture map of Ohio

Overleaf: The Olentangy River, north of Columbus

5

"*Beautiful Ohio*"

"Beautiful Ohio"

O hio is great, but it isn't very big. The Buckeye State covers 41,330 square miles. Only fifteen of the other forty-nine states are smaller.

Five states and two major bodies of water border Ohio. Pennsylvania is to the east. Indiana is Ohio's neighbor to the west. Michigan is to the north. Also to the north is Lake Erie. It is one of the five Great Lakes at the United States-Canada border. To the south are West Virginia and Kentucky. The Ohio River separates these states from southern Ohio.

The Miami, Scioto, and Muskingum rivers flow into the Ohio River. The Maumee, Sandusky, and Cuyahoga rivers run into Lake Erie. The largest lake within the state is Grand Lake. It was formed by dams on two creeks. Bass, bluegills, and catfish swim in the state's rivers and lakes.

Of its nearly 1,000-mile length, the Ohio River flows for about 450 miles along the Ohio border.

Bur marigolds in a meadow near Ladue Reservoir

"Beautiful Ohio" is the state song. It is a fitting title. Ohio is largely a land of lovely hills and valleys. Farmland covers more than half the state. Forests cover about a quarter of Ohio. Ohio's trees include black walnuts, hickories, maples, oaks, and beeches. Deer and foxes live in the woodlands.

Beautiful Ohio has a pleasant climate. In summer, the temperature often reaches above 80 degrees Fahrenheit. In winter, the temperature stays around 30 degrees Fahrenheit. But on February 10, 1899, it dropped to minus 39 degrees Fahrenheit at Milligan. About 2.5 feet of snow falls each year on the state.

Above left: Ash Cave, in the Hocking Hills

White-tailed deer

9

From Ancient Times Until Today

From Ancient Times Until Today

S hallow seas and swamps covered Ohio millions of years ago. When the seas dried, they left behind salt and limestone. When the swamps drained, coal and oil were left behind.

About 2 million years ago, the Ice Age began. Glaciers covered most of Ohio. These ice sheets spread rich soil across most of the state. This helped make Ohio a great farming region. The glaciers also scooped holes in the ground. Later, the holes filled with water. They became the Great Lakes as well as many smaller lakes.

American Indians

Ancient Indians reached Ohio about 10,000 years ago. The Ice Age was just ending. Those early Ohioans hunted mastodons and mammoths with spears.

About 3,000 years ago, American Indians began building dirt mounds. More than 10,000 mounds have been found in Ohio. Many were cone-shaped burial mounds. Others were earth "forts" or ceremonial sites. Some were shaped like giant animals.

Opposite: Muskets being fired during a Revolutionary War reenactment at Fort Laurens, near Bolivar

Ohio Mound Builders made this bird's-claw design from mica.

Great Serpent Mound is one-fourth of a mile long.

Great Serpent Mound near Hillsboro looks like a huge snake.

By the 1700s, perhaps 20,000 Indians lived in Ohio. They included the Delaware, Shawnee, Miami, Mingo, Wyandot, and Ottawa. The Indians lived in dome-shaped huts called wigwams. They grew corn and beans and hunted deer.

FRENCH AND ENGLISH CLAIMS IN OHIO

La Salle's full name was René-Robert Cavelier, Sieur de La Salle.

French explorer La Salle was probably the first white person in Ohio. He could have arrived as early as 1669. France claimed Ohio based on his travels. Yet, France did not settle Ohio.

Meanwhile, England was settling colonies along the Atlantic Ocean. England also claimed all land west of the colonies. Soon the colonies became crowded. Colonists began looking west to Ohio. In 1747, people in England and Virginia formed the first Ohio Company. This company hoped to settle Ohio. It also hoped to trade for furs with the Indians. In 1750, the company sent Christopher Gist to explore Ohio.

Christopher Gist was born in Maryland. He was a friend of George Washington, whose life he saved at least twice.

In 1754, England and France began a war over the Ohio lands. This is called the French and Indian War. Many Indians helped France. England won the war in 1763. Ohio came under English rule.

More English fur traders arrived. They included a few from the first Ohio Company. But England built no permanent towns in Ohio. In fact, England wouldn't allow colonists to move west of the Appalachian Mountains.

THE UNITED STATES TAKES OVER

In 1775, American colonists began fighting the Revolutionary War. They wanted to break free from England. Much frontier fighting occurred in Ohio. In 1780, George Rogers Clark won the Battle of Piqua. He led Americans against Shawnee Indians.

They were helping the English. Some claim that Clark won the Ohio country for the United States.

The Americans won the war in 1783. The thirteen colonies had become the United States of America. The United States gained all English land east of the Mississippi River and north of Spanish Florida. In 1787, Ohio became part of the Northwest Territory. It was not yet a state.

The second Ohio Company was formed in 1786 to create the first settlement in Ohio. It had more success than the first Ohio Company. Rufus Putnam was placed in charge of the Ohio settlement. In 1788, Putnam led about fifty men into southeastern Ohio. They were from New England. On April 7, they founded Marietta. This was Ohio's first permanent non-Indian town.

Thousands of people settled in Ohio in the late 1700s. They came from the eastern states as well as from Kentucky. Once there, they cleared the fields of trees. The settlers then planted corn and wheat. The trees were used to build cabins. They also founded new towns. Cincinnati was begun in late 1788. Cleveland, Dayton, and Youngstown came soon afterward.

The Indians grew angry as settlers took their land. Miami chief Little Turtle and other Indian

This stockade called Campus Martius was one of the first structures in the new town of Marietta.

The Northwest Territory Land Office, in Marietta

14

leaders struck back. They led several successful attacks on army posts. But on August 20, 1794, General "Mad" Anthony Wayne defeated the Indians. The battle took place in a field of fallen trees. It was called the Battle of Fallen Timbers. Within twenty years, most of the Indians had been pushed out of Ohio.

THE SEVENTEENTH STATE

By 1803, Ohio had about 70,000 settlers—enough for statehood. The United States government made Ohio the seventeenth state on March 1, 1803. This is why Ohio's state flag contains seventeen stars.

Left: General Wayne at the Battle of Fallen Timbers.
Right: A copy of the blockhouse at Fort Recovery, a fort built by Wayne in 1793. Wayne was called "Mad" Anthony because he took great risks in battle.

Above: Ohio's first statehouse, in Chillicothe
Below: Oliver Hazard Perry writing his famous message: "We have met the enemy and they are ours."

Chillicothe was the first state capital (1803-1810). Later, the capital was moved to Zanesville (1810-1812). Then, it returned to Chillicothe (1812-1816). Columbus finally became the permanent capital in 1816.

In 1803, the United States bought France's land west of the Mississippi River. Ohio farmers then shipped crops to New Orleans. Shipbuilding was important in early Ohio.

Ohio played an important part in the War of 1812 (1812-1815). This war was between the United States and England. They fought over control of ocean shipping and of the Great Lakes. The Battle of Lake Erie was fought off Ohio's shore. On September 10, 1813, Oliver Hazard Perry's fleet

captured six British ships. Afterward, Perry sent the famous message: "We have met the enemy and they are ours."

But the big story in the new state was its fast growth. With the war's end, more settlers rushed into Ohio. They came by boat along the Ohio River and Lake Erie. They came by wagon along the National Road. It passed through the middle of Ohio. In the 1830s, railroads also started bringing newcomers to Ohio. From 1803 to 1850, Ohio's population rose from almost 70,000 to 1,980,329.

ANTISLAVERY ACTIVITY AND CIVIL WAR

By the early 1800s, most black people in the South were slaves. Ohio and the other northern states did not allow slavery. In fact, Ohio was the site of several "firsts" in black history.

Oberlin College opened in 1833. It was one of the first United States colleges to admit blacks. John M. Langston was an Oberlin graduate. In 1855, he was elected clerk of an Ohio township. Langston was the first black person in the country elected to office. Wilberforce University was founded in 1856. Today, it is the country's oldest mainly black private university.

Oliver Hazard Perry

Oberlin (below) was the first college in the country to admit women.

Two of Ohio's Underground Railroad "stations" were Judge Piatt's log cabin, near West Liberty (above), and the John Rankin house, in Ripley (below).

Many Ohioans worked to end slavery in the South. In 1817, Charles Osborne began the *Philanthropist* at Point Pleasant. It was the country's first antislavery newspaper.

Ohioans also helped slaves escape along the Underground Railroad. This was a series of hiding places. Slaves used them while fleeing to Canada. The John Rankin house in Ripley was a famous Underground Railroad "station." Reverend Rankin sheltered more than 2,000 escaped slaves between 1825 and 1865.

Harriet Beecher Stowe lived in Cincinnati for many years. She wrote the famous antislavery novel

Uncle Tom's Cabin. A well-known part of the book tells of slaves crossing the frozen Ohio River.

In 1861, the North and the South went to war. This was the Civil War (1861-1865). It was fought over slavery and other matters. About 345,000 Ohioans fought for the North. Ohioans Ulysses S. Grant and William T. Sherman were great northern generals. Another Ohio war hero was nine-year-old Johnny Clem. He ran away from his home in Newark, Ohio. Johnny served as a drummer boy. He bravely played his drum in battle. In one battle, he even shot a southern officer. He became known as Johnny Shiloh because of his bravery at the Battle of Shiloh (1862) in Tennessee.

In July 1863, General John Hunt Morgan led more than 2,000 southern soldiers into Ohio. About half of them were captured. The war ended in 1865. The South surrendered to General Grant. The northern victory made it possible to end slavery in the United States.

THE GROWTH OF INDUSTRY AND INVENTIONS

Ohio had everything industry needed. The state was rich in iron, coal, oil, and gas. It had a big work force. By 1860, only New York and Pennsylvania

Harriet Beecher Stowe

Johnny Clem

had more people. Ohio also had a good transportation network. By the 1860s, Ohio had more miles of railroad than any other state. Ohio helped the United States become a manufacturing giant in the late 1800s.

Ohio cities became famous for certain products. B. F. Goodrich began a rubber factory in Akron in 1870. Akron became known as the "Rubber Capital of the World." Toledo became the "Glass Capital of the World." Cincinnati helped keep Americans clean by making soap. Youngstown made steel. Cleveland refined oil. In 1870, John D. Rockefeller formed the famous Standard Oil Company in Cleveland.

Many of America's greatest inventors lived in Dayton. Today, millions of stores use cash registers. James Ritty of Dayton invented the cash register in 1879. John Patterson of Dayton bought Ritty's firm in 1884. He turned it into the famous National Cash Register Company (NCR).

Wilbur and Orville Wright, also of Dayton, made bicycles. Then, they started building flying machines. In 1903, they made the world's first airplane flight.

Ohioans also helped develop the automobile. Early cars were started with a crank. This was hard and dangerous. Charles F. Kettering (1876-1958)

The first cash register was invented by James Ritty.

20

of Loudonville invented the "self-starter" in 1909. Cars could then be started with a key instead of a crank. In 1910, Kettering founded a company that is now known as Delco.

WORLD WARS, BOOM, AND DEPRESSION

The United States entered World War I (1914-1918) in 1917. About 250,000 Ohioans helped win the war. Eddie Rickenbacker was a flyer from Columbus. He was the top United States air "ace" of the war. "Captain Eddie" shot down twenty-two enemy planes. Ohio's factories turned out airplanes, trucks, rubber, and steel for the war.

Eddie Rickenbacker (below) was a World War I air ace. To be an "ace," a flyer must shoot down at least five enemy aircraft.

During the Great Depression, these unemployed men on their way to Washington were served a meal in Cleveland.

Lillian Gish

After the war, Ohio enjoyed good times. That was during the "Roaring Twenties." Business boomed. Ohio's Warren Harding moved into the White House (1921-1923). Lillian and Dorothy Gish were among the country's brightest movie stars. They were Ohio-born sisters.

In 1929, the country ran into hard times. This was the start of the Great Depression (1929-1939). Ohio families lost their farms. Factories closed throughout the state. By 1933, nearly half of Ohio's workers didn't have jobs.

In 1941, the United States entered World War II (1939-1945). This helped end the depression. More than 800,000 Ohio men and women served their country. Ohio-made aircraft and steel also helped win the war.

PROGRESS AND PROBLEMS

In 1958, Lewis Research Center in Cleveland became part of NASA. NASA is the country's space agency. Lewis does rocket research. Work done at the center helped push the country into the space age.

Ohio astronaut Neil Armstrong (on the left) helps Edwin Aldrin place a flag on the moon in July 1969.

An Ohio-born astronaut became the first American to orbit the earth. John Glenn did this on February 20, 1962. Another Ohio astronaut, Neil Armstrong, went to the moon. On July 20, 1969, Armstrong made the first moon walk. From the moon, Armstrong said: "That's one small step for man, one giant leap for mankind."

Down on earth, the 1960s and 1970s were troubled times for America. The country fought the Vietnam War (1965-1973). There were antiwar protests across the country. On May 4, 1970, National Guardsmen fired on war protesters. This happened at Kent State University near Akron. Four students were killed.

By the 1960s, Ohio had serious pollution problems. Ohio's many cities and factories were ruining its waters. Cleveland's Cuyahoga River was full of flammable waste. In 1969, it caught fire. Lake Erie was so dirty that fish were dying in it. People couldn't swim in it because it was unhealthy.

Ohio's cities were also suffering. By the 1960s, the cities had areas that were mainly poor and black. The poor people did not have good jobs and housing. They also had little voice in government. Riots occurred in an all-black part of Cleveland in 1966. Whole blocks were burned. Several people died.

Meanwhile, many city people were moving to the suburbs. Cleveland's population was cut in half between 1950 and 1990. Other Ohio cities also lost population. Many companies left the state during the 1970s and 1980s. Ohio and nearby states became known as the "Rust Belt." It was called this because factories stood empty and rusting. Ohioans have attacked their problems, however. Progress has been made in cleaning up Ohio's air and water. Lake Erie and the Cuyahoga River are now clean enough for people and fish.

Cleveland's race relations also improved. Carl Stokes was elected mayor in 1967. Stokes became the first black mayor of a big United States city. Many other black Ohioans have since been elected

National Guard officers check a burned-out store during the 1966 riots in Cleveland.

to office. By 1992, 14 of the 132 members of the Ohio legislature were black.

Akron no longer is the Rubber Capital. Yet, it has bounced back. So have other Ohio cities. Many Ohio companies now make machinery and plastics. Cleveland has enjoyed a building boom. People have even begun to call Cleveland the "Comeback City."

Ohio still faces big problems. Air and hazardous-waste pollution must be controlled. Poverty and joblessness are big problems, too. As of 1992, one Ohio child in five was living in poverty. Ohioans hope to solve these problems by March 1, 2003. The Buckeye State will be 200 years old then. A clean, well-run Ohio would be a great birthday gift for all Buckeyes.

Cleveland's Cuyahoga River (above) caught fire in 1969.

Ohioans and Their Work

OHIOANS AND THEIR WORK

As of 1990, 10,847,115 people lived in Ohio. Only six of the other forty-nine states had more people. Candidates for president spend much time in Ohio. The state's large number of voters is one reason for this. Another reason is that Ohio is like a small United States. Candidates who do well in Ohio usually do well throughout the country.

Three-fourths of all Ohioans live in urban areas. They live in or near cities. One-fourth of Ohioans live in rural areas. They live in small towns and on farms. Of every 100 Ohioans, 88 are white and 10 are black. All these numbers closely match those for the country as a whole.

Ohioans do differ from Americans as a whole in some ways. Of every 100 Americans, 10 are Hispanic and 3 are Asian. But only 1 Ohioan in 100 is Hispanic or Asian.

Many white Ohioans have English, Irish, Welsh, German, Swedish, or Finnish backgrounds. Other families came from Italy, Greece, Yugoslavia, Poland, Slovenia, Russia, Czechoslovakia, or Hungary.

Crowds of Ohioans enjoy Cincinnati's Oktoberfest.

A member of the Dayton Pipe Band

27

BUCKEYES ON THE JOB

Some states are famous for farming. Others are best known for manufacturing. Still others are known for mining. Ohio is one of a few states that leads in all three areas.

Ohio has about 5 million workers. More than 1 million of them make products in factories. Cars and trucks are Ohio's top products. The only state ahead of Ohio at making cars is Michigan. Ohioans also make boats, bicycles, and car parts.

Machinery is Ohio's second-leading product. The state leads the country at making household appliances. Many refrigerators, stoves, and washing machines are made in Ohio. The state ranks high at making steel, tires, and paint. Packaged foods and silverware are also made in Ohio. The famous soap company Proctor & Gamble is based in Cincinnati. Ohio also has many toy companies. Cincinnati's Kenner products makes the Baby Alive doll. The Ohio Art Company at Bryan makes Etch A Sketch.

Ohio is among the top ten states at making many other goods. They include furniture, paper, books, plastics, glass, and glassware.

About 700,000 Buckeyes work for the government. These government workers include teachers.

A water-safety instructor in Rio Grande

A policeman directing traffic in Athens

Ohio has one of the country's largest public-school networks. It also has one of the largest state universities. Ohio State University at Columbus has 60,000 students.

More than 1 million Ohioans do service work. They include doctors, hotel workers, and people who service cars. About 1 million Buckeyes also sell goods.

About 125,000 Ohioans work on farms. Corn and soybeans are Ohio's leading farm products. Grapes, tomatoes, cucumbers, strawberries, and apples are other important crops. Ohio is also a top producer of eggs, milk, hogs, and horses.

About 18,000 Buckeyes earn their livings by mining. Ohio ranks ninth at producing coal. The state is a big producer of natural gas and oil. Ohio ranks near the top at producing salt.

Left: An Amish farmer cutting wheat with a four-horse team
Right: A steelworker

Below: A young girl feeds milk to a calf on an Ohio farm.
Ohio has about 80,000 farms. Only six states have more.

A Trip Through the Buckeye State

A Trip Through the Buckeye State

O hio is a great place to visit. The Buckeye State has five presidents' homes. Ohio also has Indian relics and large cities. Ohio's hills and river valleys are among America's prettiest.

SOUTHEAST OHIO

Marietta is the state's oldest town. It is a good place to begin an Ohio tour. Marietta lies along the Ohio River near Ohio's southeast corner. Rufus Putnam founded Marietta in 1788. He and others built Fort Campus Martius. Today, the Campus Martius Museum is there. It has displays on pioneer life. Rufus Putnam's wooden house is on the museum's grounds. The house dates from 1788. It is the oldest known pioneer home in Ohio.

Zanesville is northwest of Marietta. Ebenezer Zane began the town in 1797. Zane Grey (1872-1939) was born in Zanesville. This well-known writer of Western stories was Ebenezer's great-great-grandson. As a boy, Grey wrote his first story in a cave near his home.

Pages 30-31: The Columbus skyline and Scioto River

This Y bridge in Zanesville was built at the junction of the Muskingum and Licking rivers.

The National Road reached Zanesville in 1826. The National Road-Zane Grey Museum is near Zanesville. It has a model of this pioneer road. It also has displays on Zane Grey's life.

Adena State Memorial, near Chillicothe, was the home of Thomas Worthington, Ohio's sixth governor.

Chillicothe is west of Marietta. In 1803, Chillicothe became Ohio's first state capital. Thomas Worthington's hilltop mansion called Adena is there. Worthington was a leader in the work to make Ohio a state. Later, he governed Ohio (1814-1818). Today, his home is open to visitors.

North of Chillicothe are twenty-three burial mounds. They belong to the ancient Hopewell Indians. The mounds are in Mound City Group

33

National Monument. Pipes and beads have been found at the mounds.

Between Chillicothe and Marietta is Wayne National Forest. Visitors use its lake, rivers, and trails each year.

SOUTHWEST OHIO

Cincinnati lies on the Ohio River near Ohio's southwest corner. It is called the "Queen City." Cincinnati is Ohio's oldest major city. The town was settled in 1788. Today, Cincinnati is Ohio's third-largest city. It is the world's leading maker of soap. Cincinnati leads United States cities at making playing cards and machine tools.

The Taft Museum

The Cincinnati skyline

President Taft's birthplace is in Cincinnati. Much of the furniture in the home belonged to Taft's family. Taft grew up to be the biggest president. He weighed about 350 pounds.

Cincinnati also has one of the country's best zoos. The Cincinnati Zoo is known for its cat collection. It includes white Bengal tigers. The zoo is also home to Insect World. This is the only insect house in a United States zoo.

The Cincinnati Art Museum has works dating back to ancient Egypt. The Cincinnati Museum of Natural History has displays on Ice Age animals. Visitors can walk through its life-size cave.

Sports fans fill Riverfront Stadium. The Bengals play pro football there. It is also home to the Reds. That is Cincinnati's pro baseball team. That team has won five World Series (1919, 1940, 1975, and 1990).

Fort Ancient is northeast of Cincinnati. This earthwork ceremonial site was built by ancient Hopewell Indians. It is one of the country's largest ancient Indian structures. Fort Ancient was built about 2,000 years ago.

Dayton is north of Fort Ancient. Settlers arrived there on April 1, 1796. Today, Dayton is Ohio's sixth-largest city.

A camel ride at the Cincinnati Zoo

Riverfront Stadium

An early Wright brothers military airplane as well as modern military aircraft are on display at the United States Air Force Museum near Dayton.

Wright-Patterson Air Force Base is near Dayton. A field where the Wright brothers tested airplanes is part of the base. The United States Air Force Museum is at the base. An early Wright brothers airplane can be seen there. The Wright brothers built early airplanes in a bicycle shop in Dayton. The shop was later moved to Dearborn, Michigan.

The Paul Laurence Dunbar House is also in Dayton. Dunbar, a great black poet, was born in Dayton. Visitors can see his papers. His other belongings include a Wright brothers bicycle.

Nearby is Wilberforce, Ohio. The National Afro-American Museum and Cultural Center is there. It is a fine place to learn about black history.

COLUMBUS, THE STATE CAPITAL

Columbus is in the center of Ohio. The city has been Ohio's capital since 1816. With more than 630,000 people, Columbus is also Ohio's largest city. Ohio lawmakers meet in the state capitol in Columbus. This beautiful building was finished in 1861. Visitors can watch the legislature at work. Many people in Columbus work for the government. Others work for Ohio State University. That school is home to the Buckeye sports teams.

Ohio Village is a highlight of Columbus. It has been built to look like an 1860s Ohio town. The people who work there dress in clothing from Civil

A statue of President William McKinley stands in front of the capitol in Columbus.

The capitol

Ohio Caverns

An F50 Skylancer at the Neil Armstrong Air and Space Museum in Wapakoneta

War times. They show visitors how the settlers made cloth, horseshoes, and tools.

NORTHWEST OHIO

Northwest of Columbus, there are caves to explore. Ohio Caverns is the state's largest known cave. Nearby Zane Caverns has rare cave pearls. They are small, round, polished formations of calcite. Cave pearls are smoothed by the motion of the water in some cave pools.

Northwest of the caves is Wapakoneta. The Neil Armstrong Air and Space Museum is at Wapakoneta. Neil Armstrong was born in that town in 1930. In 1969, he was the first person on the moon. The museum has a moon rock that Armstrong brought back.

Northeast of Wapakoneta is Toledo. It is the state's fourth-largest city. Toledo lies along Lake Erie. The town was begun in 1817. In the 1880s, Toledo became well known for making glass. Today, Toledo is a major center for making auto parts.

Visitors enjoy the Toledo Museum of Art. It has a large glass collection. The Toledo Zoo has the world's only underwater hippoquarium. There, people watch hippopotamuses play.

Sandusky is east of Toledo along Lake Erie. Cedar Point Amusement Park is at Sandusky. It has fifty-five rides and ten water slides.

North of Sandusky are some islands. They are in the part of Lake Erie that belongs to Ohio. They include Kelleys Island and the three Bass Islands. The islands are popular vacation spots. Inscription Rock is on Kelleys Island. It has 400-year-old Indian carvings.

Southeast of Sandusky is Milan. The Thomas Edison Birthplace Museum is in Milan. Edison lived there for his first seven years. The house has a few of Edison's inventions.

A view of Put-In-Bay on South Bass Island

The Thomas Edison Birthplace, in Milan

39

A statue of General Moses Cleaveland, founder of Cleveland

A view of Cleveland

NORTHEAST OHIO

Cleveland is Ohio's second-biggest city. The city sits where the Cuyahoga River flows into Lake Erie. Cleveland got its name through a spelling mistake. In 1796, Moses Cleaveland founded the town. It was named for him. In 1831, a newspaper left off the first a. Ever since, it has been spelled *Cleveland* instead of *Cleaveland*. Today, cars and airplane parts are made in Cleveland. The city's port is one of Lake Erie's busiest.

Downtown Cleveland has been improved since the 1980s. New restaurants and shops have opened along the Cuyahoga River. In 1985, the forty-six-

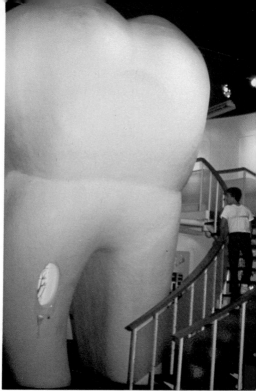

story Standard Oil headquarters was finished. It is now called the BP America Building. Cleveland's tallest building is the fifty-seven-story Society Center. It measures 948 feet to the top of the spire. Society Center is also Ohio's tallest building.

Cleveland has many museums. The Cleveland Museum of Natural History has dinosaur fossils. The Cleveland Museum of Art has artworks from almost every country. The Cleveland Health Education Museum has a giant-sized tooth. Visitors can walk through it.

A new kind of music was born in America during the 1950s. In 1951, Cleveland radio announcer Alan Freed named it "rock and roll." The Rock and

Roll Hall of Fame is scheduled to open in Cleveland in 1995. It will honor the great rock and roll stars.

The Cleveland Orchestra is one of the world's best. Karamu House and Theatre is well-known. Its plays and dances help people of different races understand one another.

Cleveland has three pro sports teams. The Indians play baseball. The Browns play football. Basketball fans enjoy the Cleveland Cavaliers.

Three big cities form a triangle south of Cleveland. One of them is Akron. It was founded in 1825. Akron became well known for its rubber goods. Stan Hywet Hall is an Akron landmark. This sixty-five-room mansion was F. A. Seiberling's

Akron means "high point" in Greek. The city is on high land.

Stan Hywet Hall, in Akron, was the home of F. A. Seiberling, founder of the Goodyear Tire & Rubber Company.

Lanterman's Mill, in Youngstown

home. Seiberling founded the Goodyear Tire & Rubber Company in 1898. Goodyear blimps are often seen flying over sporting events.

Today, Akron is Ohio's fifth-biggest city. It has become a major plastics-making center. Little Tikes is near Akron. It is one of the country's leading makers of plastic toys.

Each summer, Akron hosts the All-American Soap Box Derby. "Soap boxes" are homemade cars with no motors. Young people nine through sixteen years old race cars in this event.

Soap boxes travel by going downhill.

Youngstown is the second city in the triangle. It is east of Akron. Youngstown was once a great steel-

43

The Professional Football Hall of Fame is in Canton.

making city. Today, Youngstown's factories make many different kinds of goods. Some of them are light bulbs, paints, paper, clothes, and cars. Youngstown also has the Butler Institute of American Art. It was the gift of steel-maker Joseph Butler.

Canton completes the triangle. Canton is south of Akron. It has always been an important steel-making city. William McKinley made his home in Canton. He worked as a lawyer there before becoming president. In 1901, President McKinley was shot and killed. He is buried at the McKinley Memorial in Canton.

Canton was also home to an early pro football team. It was called the Canton Bulldogs. Jim Thorpe played for the Bulldogs. He was one of America's greatest athletes. In 1920, the National Football League (NFL) was begun in Canton. Today, the Pro Football Hall of Fame is there. It is a good place to learn about football history.

Zoar Village is a perfect place to end an Ohio trip. It is a quiet spot south of Canton. People from Germany founded this little village in 1817. They were seeking religious freedom. The people of the village shared the work. Zoar Village looks much as it did in the 1800s.

The Garden House and Green House in historic Zoar Village

Overleaf: Annie Oakley

A Gallery of Famous Buckeyes

A GALLERY OF FAMOUS BUCKEYES

O hio, we know, has produced more than its share of presidents and inventors. But many other famous people have also been Ohioans. They include children's authors, baseball players, and movie stars.

Two famous Shawnee Indian brothers were Ohioans. **Tecumseh** (1768-1813) and **Tenskwatawa** (1775?-1834) were born near present-day Dayton. They tried to bring Indian groups together to fight the white settlers. Tenskwatawa also tried to get Indians to go back to their old ways. In 1811, Tenskwatawa lost the Battle of Tippecanoe in Indiana. This ended the plan for a united Indian group.

John Chapman (1774-1845) planted apple seeds in Ohio. People called him "Johnny Appleseed." Chapman planted about 1,200 acres of trees.

William Tecumseh Sherman (1820-1891) was born in Lancaster. He was named for the Shawnee chief. Tecumseh was a friend of his father's. Sherman became one of the North's most famous Civil War generals.

Tecumseh

General William Tecumseh Sherman

Left to right: Ulysses Grant, William McKinley, William Howard Taft
Below: Rutherford B. Hayes

After the Civil War, several Ohioans served as president of the United States. **Ulysses S. Grant** (1822-1885) of Point Pleasant served from 1869 to 1877. From 1877 to 1881, **Rutherford B. Hayes** (1822-1893) of Delaware, Ohio, was president. **James A. Garfield** (1831-1881) of Orange served for a few months in 1881. He was shot and died in office. **Benjamin Harrison** (1833-1901) of North Bend was president from 1889 to 1893. **William McKinley** (1843-1901) of Niles also was shot and died in office. He served as president from 1897 to 1901. **William H. Taft** (1857-1930) of Cincinnati was president from 1909 to 1913. **Warren G.**

Harding (1865-1923) of Blooming Grove served from 1921 to 1923). He, too, died in office.

Annie Oakley (1860-1926) was born in Patterson. She learned to shoot a gun as a child. Oakley helped pay for her family's farm. She sold meat from animals she had shot. Oakley was a member of Buffalo Bill Cody's Wild West Show (1885-1902). She was a sharpshooter. One of her tricks was to shoot a cigarette from her husband's mouth.

Thomas Edison (1847-1931) was born in Milan, Ohio. He later worked in New Jersey. Edison invented the record player in 1877. He made his greatest invention, the electric light, in 1879.

Ransom Olds (1864-1950) was born in Geneva, Ohio. He made some of the world's first

Thomas Alva Edison

Ransom Olds is on the right, holding his hat.

Toni Morrison

cars. In 1899, he founded the Olds Motor Works in Detroit, Michigan. This factory made Oldsmobiles. They were named for him.

Ohio has produced many great authors. **Sherwood Anderson** (1876-1941) was born in Camden. He ran a paint factory in Elyria, near Cleveland. One day, Anderson walked out of the factory. He wanted to be a writer. He wrote *Winesburg, Ohio.* It is about a fictional Ohio town.

Toni Morrison was born in 1931 in Lorain. Her book *Beloved* won the 1988 Pulitzer Prize for fiction. In 1993, Morrison became the first black American to win the Nobel Prize for literature.

The Caldecott Medal is given yearly to an artist of children's books. **Robert McCloskey** was born in Hamilton in 1914. He has won two Caldecotts. *Make Way for Ducklings* won in 1942. *Time of Wonder* was the 1958 winner.

Each year, an author of books for young people wins the Newbery Medal. Springfield native **Lois Lenski** (1893-1974) won the 1946 Newbery for *Strawberry Girl.* **Virginia Hamilton** won the 1975 Newbery for *M. C. Higgins, the Great.* She was born in Yellow Springs in 1936. **Robin McKinley** was born in Warren in 1952. She won the 1985 Newbery for *The Hero and the Crown.*

John Glenn was born in 1921 in Cambridge. He was an astronaut. In 1962, he became the first American to orbit the earth. Later, he became a lawmaker. Since 1975, Glenn has represented Ohio in the U.S. Senate.

Carl Stokes was born in Cleveland in 1927. His father died when he was two. Carl's mother worked as a cleaning woman to support the family. Stokes became a lawyer. He was mayor of Cleveland from 1967 to 1971. Stokes was the first black mayor of a big American city.

Many great athletes have been Buckeyes. The Cy Young Award goes to baseball's finest pitchers. It was named for Gilmore native **Denton True "Cy" Young** (1867-1955). Young won thirty-two or more games in five separate seasons. His 511 wins are the most by a big-league pitcher. **Pete Rose** was born in Cincinnati in 1941. He was a star with the Cincinnati Reds. Rose holds the record for the most career hits—4,256. Rose won three bat-

Left: Carl Stokes, on the right, taking the oath of office
Right: Cy Young

Pete Rose

Clark Gable

Margaret Hamilton

ting crowns along the way. **Mike Schmidt** was born in Dayton in 1949. He, too, became a great ballplayer. Schmidt hit 548 home runs. That's a record for a third baseman.

Quarterback **Roger Staubach** was born in Cincinnati in 1942. His passing helped the Dallas Cowboys win two Super Bowls (1972 and 1978).

The famous golfer **Jack Nicklaus** was born in Columbus in 1940. His nickname is the "Golden Bear." Nicklaus is golf's leading money winner.

Maya Ying Lin was born in Athens, Ohio, in 1959. This Asian-American woman designed the Vietnam Veterans Memorial in Washington, D.C. She was only twenty-one years old at the time.

Movie star **Clark Gable** (1901-1960) was born in Cadiz. Gable's best-known role was Rhett Butler in *Gone With the Wind.* In 1934, he won an Academy Award for best actor. That was for his role in *It Happened One Night.* Actress **Margaret Hamilton** (1902-1985) was born in Cleveland. She played the Wicked Witch of the West in *The Wizard of Oz.* Before becoming a famous actress, she taught nursery school. **Paul Newman** was born in Shaker Heights in 1925. In 1986, he won the Academy Award for best actor. It was for his role in *The Color of Money.*

Jack Nicklaus

Steven Spielberg was born in Cincinnati in 1947. In his youth, Spielberg made horror movies. They starred his three younger sisters. Spielberg became a famous movie director. He made *Jaws, E.T.,* and *Raiders of the Lost Ark.*

Steven Spielberg

The birthplace of Tecumseh, Neil Armstrong, Maya Ying Lin, Paul Laurence Dunbar, Annie Oakley, and Thomas Edison . . .

Mother of Presidents and of Inventors . . .

A big producer of plastics, soaps, rubber goods, cars, coal, steel, eggs, and salt . . .

Site of Zoar Village, the Pro Football Hall of Fame, and Great Serpent Mound . . .

This is Ohio—the Buckeye State!

Did You Know?

It is not known whether the expression "Holy Toledo!" refers to Toledo, Ohio, or Toledo, Spain. If it refers to Toledo, Ohio, it may be because of the city's many churches.

Cedar Point Amusement Park in Sandusky has the world's tallest wooden roller coaster. The Mean Streak stands sixteen stories high and reaches speeds of 65 miles per hour.

Joe Nuxhall of the Cincinnati Reds was the youngest big-league player in history. Nuxhall pitched for the Reds in 1944 when he was only fifteen years old.

Dorothy Kamenshek, of Norwood, was the All-Time Batting Leader of the All-American Girls Professional Baseball League, which existed from 1943 to 1954. Kamenshek's team was called the Rockford Peaches.

In 1879, Cleveland became the first United States city to have electric street lights. When the city's lights first went on, some people closed their eyes. They feared that the lights would blind them.

Ohio is one of the few states with towns that start with every letter of the alphabet. Towns starting with Q, X, and Z are usually hard to find. But Ohio has Quaker City, Quincy, Xenia, Zaleski, and Zanesville.

Ohio also has towns named Buckeye Lake, Magnetic Springs, Mount Healthy, Reminderville, and Risingsun.

The United States record for returning an overdue book is 145 years. The book was taken from a Cincinnati library in 1823 and returned by the borrower's great-grandson in 1968. The fine was figured at $2,264. The great-grandson was not made to pay, however.

One night, ten-year-old Becky Schroeder of Toledo was waiting for her mother in a parked car. She wanted to do her homework, but it was too dark. By the age of twelve, Becky had invented Glo-Sheet. It lights up papers placed on it. Within a few years, Becky had sold Glo-Sheet to police departments, hospitals, and even the United States Navy.

In 1893, Mount Union College in Alliance became one of the country's first colleges to form a basketball team.

OHIO INFORMATION

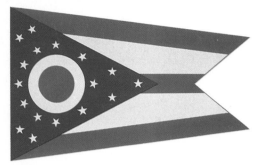

State flag

Ohio buckeye

Area: 41,330 square miles (only fifteen states are smaller)

Greatest Distance North to South: 210 miles

Greatest Distance East to West: 230 miles

Borders: Pennsylvania to the east; Indiana to the west; Michigan and Lake Erie to the north; West Virginia and Kentucky to the south

Highest Point: Campbell Hill, northwest of Columbus, 1,550 feet above sea level

Lowest Point: 433 feet above sea level, in the state's southwest corner

Hottest Recorded Temperature: 113° F. (at Thurman, on July 4, 1897, and near Gallipolis, on July 21, 1934)

Coldest Recorded Temperature: -39° F. (at Milligan, on February 10, 1899)

Statehood: The seventeenth state, on March 1, 1803

Origin of Name: *Ohio* is an Indian word meaning "something great"

Capital: Columbus (since 1816)

Previous Capitals: Chillicothe (1803-1810 and 1812-1816), Zanesville (1810-1812)

Counties: 88

United States Senators: 2

United States Representatives: 19 (as of 1992)

State Senators: 33

State Representatives: 99

State Song: "Beautiful Ohio" by Ballard MacDonald (words) and Mary Earl (music)

State Motto: "With God, All Things Are Possible"

Main Nickname: "Buckeye State"

Other Nicknames: "Mother of Presidents," "Mother of Inventors"

State Seal: Adopted in 1967

State Flag: Adopted in 1902

State Flower: Scarlet carnation

State Bird: Cardinal

State Tree: Buckeye

State Insect: Ladybug

State Stone: Flint

State Drink: Tomato juice

Some Rivers: Ohio, Scioto, Muskingum, Great Miami, Little Miami, Maumee, Sandusky, Cuyahoga

Some Lakes: Erie, Grand, Berlin, Indian

Wildlife: Deer, foxes, muskrats, raccoons, coyotes, minks, opossums, rabbits, skunks, bald eagles, ducks, geese, quails, cardinals, chickadees, catfish, perch, pike, bass, turtles

Manufactured Products: Cars, trucks, car and airplane parts, household appliances and other machinery, steel and many metal goods, packaged meat, baked goods, dairy goods, soap, chemicals, tires and other rubber goods, plastics, paint, toys, sporting goods, furniture, paper, newspapers, books, magazines, hand tools, glass and glassware, plumbing and heating equipment, farm and garden equipment, construction equipment

Farm Products: Corn, soybeans, eggs, milk, chickens, hogs and pigs, horses and ponies, sheep, beef cattle, grapes, oats, tomatoes, cucumbers, strawberries, apples, tobacco, popcorn

Mining Products: Coal, natural gas, oil, salt, clay, limestone, sandstone, sand and gravel, gypsum

Population: 10,847,115, seventh among the fifty states (1990 U.S. Census Bureau figures)

Major Cities (1990 Census):

Columbus	632,910
Cleveland	505,616
Cincinnati	364,040
Toledo	332,943
Akron	223,019
Dayton	182,044
Youngstown	95,732

Cardinal

Ladybugs

Mink

Ohio History

8000 B.C.—Prehistoric Indians reach Ohio about this time

1669—French explorer René-Robert Cavelier, Sieur de La Salle, is thought to have traveled along the Ohio River

1750—Christopher Gist explores Ohio for the first Ohio Company

1763—England wins the French and Indian War against France; Ohio comes under English rule

1775-83—Americans fight the Revolutionary War and win their freedom from England

1787—Ohio becomes part of the Northwest Territory

1788—Rufus Putnam founds Marietta, Ohio's first permanent non-Indian town; Cincinnati is begun

1794—General "Mad" Anthony Wayne defeats Indians at the Battle of Fallen Timbers near present-day Toledo

1796—Cleveland and Dayton are founded

1803—Ohio becomes the seventeenth state on March 1

1813—During the War of 1812, Oliver Hazard Perry wins the Battle of Lake Erie

1816—Columbus becomes Ohio's permanent capital

1833—Oberlin College opens as the first U.S. college to admit women and blacks

1840—The National Road is completed

1851—Ohio adopts the state constitution that is in use today

1861-65—The Civil War is fought; about 345,000 Ohioans help the North win; the northern victory ends slavery in the United States

1869—Ulysses S. Grant becomes the eighteenth president of the United States; the Cincinnati Red Stockings become the first pro baseball team

1877—Rutherford B. Hayes becomes the nineteenth president of the United States

James A. Garfield, twentieth president of the United States

1879—James Ritty of Dayton invents the cash register; Ohio's Thomas Edison invents the electric light in New Jersey

1881—James A. Garfield becomes the twentieth president of the United States, making three Ohio-born presidents in a row

1889—Benjamin Harrison becomes the twenty-third president of the United States

1897—William McKinley takes office as the twenty-fifth president of the United States

1903—The Wright brothers of Dayton make the first airplane flight

1909—William H. Taft becomes the twenty-seventh president of the United States

1917-18—After the United States enters World War I, more than 250,000 Ohioans serve

1921—Warren G. Harding becomes the twenty-ninth president of the United States

1929-39—During the Great Depression, many Ohio factories and farms go out of business

1941-45—After the United States enters World War II, about 840,000 Ohioans serve

1955—The Ohio Turnpike opens

1962—Ohio astronaut John Glenn becomes the first American to orbit the earth

1967—Cleveland's Carl Stokes becomes the first black mayor of a big U.S. city

1969—Ohio astronaut Neil Armstrong becomes the first person to walk on the moon

1991—George V. Voinovich becomes Ohio's governor

Warren G. Harding, twenty-ninth president of the United States

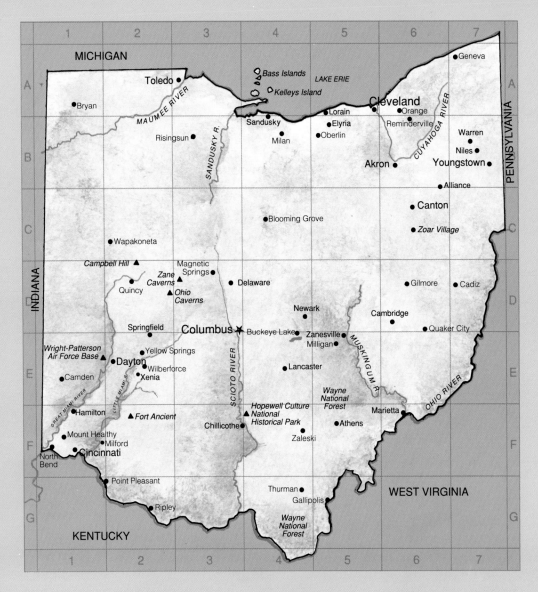

MICHIGAN

LAKE ERIE

Bryan

Toledo

Bass Islands

Kelleys Island

Geneva

Cleveland
Orange
Reminderville

Lorain
Sandusky
Elyria
Milan
Oberlin

Warren
Niles
Youngstown

Akron

Risingsun

MAUMEE RIVER

SANDUSKY R.

CUYAHOGA RIVER

PENNSYLVANIA

INDIANA

Alliance

Canton

Blooming Grove

Zoar Village

Wapakoneta

Campbell Hill

Magnetic Springs

Zane Caverns
Quincy
Ohio Caverns

Delaware

Gilmore
Cadiz

Newark

Cambridge

Columbus
Buckeye Lake
Zanesville
Milligan

Quaker City

Springfield

Wright-Patterson Air Force Base
Dayton
Yellow Springs
Wilberforce
Xenia

Lancaster

Camden

MUSKINGUM R.

SCIOTO RIVER

LITTLE MIAMI R.

GREAT MIAMI RIVER

Hamilton

Fort Ancient

Wayne National Forest

Hopewell Culture National Historical Park

Chillicothe

Athens

Marietta

OHIO RIVER

Mount Healthy
Milford
Cincinnati

Zaleski

North Bend

Point Pleasant

Thurman

WEST VIRGINIA

Ripley

Gallipolis

KENTUCKY

Wayne National Forest

GLOSSARY

ancient: Relating to a time long ago

antislavery: Against slavery

antiwar: Against war

astronaut: A person who is highly trained for spaceflight

buckeye: Another name for a horse-chestnut tree or its nutlike seeds; Ohio is called the Buckeye State and its people are called Buckeyes

candidate: A person who runs for office

capital: A city that is the seat of government

capitol: A building in which the government meets

climate: The typical weather of a region

colony: A settlement that is outside a parent country and that is ruled by the parent country

explorer: A person who visits and studies unknown lands

industry: A business that needs many workers to make products

inventor: A person who creates a new device or a new way of doing things

legislature: A lawmaking body

mammoths and mastodons: Large Ice Age animals much like the elephants of today

manufacturing: The making of products

memorial: A structure built in memory of a person

million: A thousand thousand (1,000,000)

permanent: Lasting

pioneers: A person who is among the first to move into a region

pollute: To make dirty

population: The number of people in a place

rural: Relating to farm areas and small towns

slave: A person who is owned by another person

swamp: Wet, spongy land sometimes covered by water

wigwam: An Indian home that was made of poles and covered by bark and other materials

A colorful autumn scene at Brandywine Falls, in the Cuyahoga Valley

INDEX

Page numbers in boldface type indicate illustrations.

ABOUT THE AUTHOR

Dennis Brindell Fradin is the author of 150 published children's books. His works for Childrens Press include the Young People's Stories of Our States series, the Disaster! series, and the Thirteen Colonies series. Dennis is married to Judith Bloom Fradin, who taught high-school and college English for many years. She is now Dennis's chief researcher. The Fradins are the parents of two sons, Anthony and Michael, and a daughter, Diana. Dennis graduated from Northwestern University in 1967 with a B.A. in creative writing, and has lived in Evanston, Illinois, since that year.